Skinny, Happy and Rich

Ridgely Goldsborough

Skinny, Happy and Rich
by Ridgely Goldsborough

Revised Edition. Second Printing.
ISBN 0-9745696-2-3

For additional copies, visit:
www.AViewFromTheRidge.com

Cover Design: Tammy Sadler
Photo Credit: Donald Puckett

Printed in Canada.

3

Dedication

To my love partner, Ali, who makes the Happy part possible ...

To my business partner, Sharon, who takes care of the Rich part ...

Oh, does that mean I have to do the Skinny part myself???
Oy.

Contents

PROLOGUE

We all know those people simply born thin, who grow up thin and somehow, by divine intervention, stay that way year after year, no matter what they eat or don't eat, whether they exercise or not, whether Mercury slips into retrograde or the sky falls in.

Can you picture the type?

Well, I hate them. I hate all of them—down to their unfairly skinny ankles and feet that slip perfectly into their model-size skinny shoes. I wish for once that they could wake up pudgy, struggle to stuff their bodies into last year's clothes (that used to fit passably well) and experience the perennial battle of the bulge that the rest of us less-than-humans grunt our way through every day. Then I might feel a tad more forgiving. Or not.

What about that other horrid group, the happy people, those unfazed grin-wearers that walk around in a state of perpetual rosiness, smiling at the cards life deals them, enjoying the topsy-turvy ride that we "others" painfully endure?

I hate them, too. They seem to have completely forgotten the ageless truth that misery loves company and that most of us sport our miserableness like an honorable badge, a comforting, welcome place of daily pain.

I wish we could wipe their toothy grins off the face of this planet, ban them like cigarettes in swanky California restaurants, quarantine them into designated grinning areas.

Lastly, we have the rich. I hate them the most. Since they can use their money to buy skinny and happy, they deserve to be hated above all else. How incredibly rude that they can buy a trainer and a sprout-loving organic salad tosser, spend a few shekels to acquire a passel of friends that love and adore them (or at least say they do), proclaim themselves glorious recipients of universal blessings, grateful and appreciative for their lot in life—you know, the five acre mansion encrusted piece of dirt down by the shoreline, skirted by palm trees that look like upside down feather dusters.

Who could possibly be more hate-able?

If you are already skinny, happy and rich, get out of my book. You make the rest of us uncomfortable.

If you confess a love of donuts and burgers, could take a bath in warm chocolate and not get *out until you licked yourself clean and spend more money on insufficient bank charges than yuppies throw at lattes and frappuccinos, then welcome to our world, a community of comrade frowners, ordinary earth dwellers who never second guess a double chili-dog, appreciate the value of another plate of cheap cheese and understand that as long as we have checks left in our small vinyl books, we can chase away a grimace with a frivolous purchase, then justify its familiar return when the overdrawn bank notices clog our mailbox. You've come home.*

This foreword spoofs life's most wondrous journey. There will never be an undertaking more daunting, challenging, frustrating and rewarding than the process of self-discovery, the debunking of personal myths that hinder our happiness, the cleansing of layer after layer of gunky muck. Still, the travel lightens with laughter. If you believe as I do, that the path ends only when the lights go out once and for all, then let's grow full, colorful gardens along the way, pick the weeds, sow the seeds, sing to the flowers and laugh our way all the way to the grave.

Enjoy!

Chapter One

Start
Now

Skinny, Happy and Rich

What, let go of my remote and get off of this couch?

Are you nuts? After a brutal day of clock punching at the whim of that power-mongering beast? No way, man.

Why do you think they invented chips and salsa in the first place?

Besides, Wheel of Fortune re-runs make me feel good. I know all the answers. You think I'm going to give that up because of a tired New Year's resolution made under extraordinary peer pressure? You think I'm ready to leap into an unknown abyss of painful possible failure, risk my beloved beer belly for a pie-in-the-sky upside impossible to define, difficult to measure and potentially years in the making?

Are you kidding me? Gimme' a pill and a Twinkie and step away from the screen.

Until one is committed, there is a hesitancy, the chance to draw back, always ineffectiveness. Concerning all acts of initiative and creation, there is one elementary truth, the ignorance of which kills countless pleas and splendid plans; that the moment one definitely commits oneself, then Providence moves too. All sorts of things occur to help one that would never otherwise have occurred. A whole stream of events issues from the decision, raising in one's favor all manner of unforeseen incidents and meetings and material assistance, which no man could have dreamed would have come his way.

Whatever you can do or dream you can, begin it. Boldness has Genius, Power and Magic in it.

Begin it now.

-Goethe

Sound familiar? It should. Not one of us lives without the all-too-persuasive nattering voice that yaks constantly, pours reservoirs of brackish gunk into our fragile psyches and converts our will into molasses.

"It's too hard to change."

Translation: *"I'm not willing to mobilize my sorry self and would prefer it if you didn't upset my boat."*

"Why bother? You'll fail anyway."

Translation: *"I'm scared to death to try anything new."*

"It never happens for people like us."

Translation: *"My belief in myself flushed down the toilet sometime toward the end of the last millennium."*

And so on. What trips we lay on ourselves! In the quiet, yet oddly not so relaxing recline of our favorite La-Z-Boy, we noodle possibilities,

All glory comes from daring to begin.

-*Eugene Ware*

generally declining to follow them further—especially if that pursuit would require getting out of the chair. We ogle what we want as it materializes and disappears at the flick of a television switch or the turn of a magazine page. We flirt with skittish *"what-ifs"* that dance their ways into our mental picture and grace us with a pirouette before they leap out of frame.

Or we analyze. We exhaust ourselves looking at every angle, the ups and downs, the potential risks, the personal price. We reach a state of paralysis by analysis. We can't get off the dime.

Have you ever had this internal conversation?

"It's about time I did my own thing. I am sick and tired of my pants feeling too tight and my bank account too light. I am disgusted with my acceptance of the slave labor I grind out every day. If you grind something down, it wears out. That's my life, worn to the core. It's time I propelled myself in a direction of my own choosing."

Most of us have. The challenge springs front and center in the second inner dialogue—the one that creeps into our consciousness like springtime Louisiana weeds, tenacious, rooted and virtually indestructible.

Skinny, Happy and Rich

The first rule of holes:
If you're in one, stop digging.

"Yeah, I'd really like to do something. This is getting me nowhere. If only I had the drive and the motivation, not to mention the money. If only I knew the right people, had the right education, exhibited the right personality. I could really do something."

The doubts begin, paving the way for the third brainchild, stronger and established in most cases over multiple generations.

"No way, not you. If you really could, you would have done it already. It's not like you haven't had these thoughts before. This is the same soggy, washed out idea you often visit and never live. Who are you kidding? Have another potato chip and ruminate."

We spin. We turn in a whirlpool of confusion, frustration and apprehension. We wrestle in confusion between the desire to make a change and the belief ingrained like Excalibur in the rock that we don't deserve any better. We fight the frustration of our current miserable circumstance and the constant knowing that *"Hey, this is my destiny."* We battle the apprehension of appearing the fool. In the end, we dig our heels in our own dread, anchor our pain and allow a blinding

Only those who do things get criticized.

numbness to take over, one extra inch at a time, one more lost dream.

Does it have to be that way?

No way.

Can we do it differently?

You bet.

Is it easy?

Not in a million years.

That's why so few of us are Skinny, Happy and Rich.

But it's doable—and anyone can get there.

Winning starts with beginning.

A journey of a thousand miles begins with a single step.

What, as opposed to a journey of ten miles? What about a mile and a half? How does that one kick off?

Oh, with a single step.

That's the point. We have to take our focus away from the alligators and crocodiles that inhabit our mental swamp, block out the inherited tendency to make the inevitable potholes seem more porous than the Grand Canyon and just put

One can never consent to creep
when one feels an impulse to soar.

-Helen Keller

one foot forward.

Not two feet. Not a blinding leap.

One step.

Take it. Own it. It won't bite and you'll feel better once your weight settles on the forward foot.

Few powers on earth carry the momentum of forward movement, any movement. When you take the first step, you successfully defy the prison guards within. You trample them and send them scurrying like rats in a dank warehouse after someone hits the halogen switch.

Every great endeavor has its origins in a single action. By starting, you set the wheels in motion. Whatever the mind can conceive, you can achieve.

The mighty sequoia that grows three hundred feet to caress the sky once fit in the palm of your hand. One day, braving storms and empty-bellied squirrels, it began to grow.

That seed represents your dreams.

All you have to do is start.

Even if you're on the right track,
you'll get run over if you just sit there.

-Will Rogers

Summary

- *The Skinny, Happy and Rich don't wait.*
- *They understand that nothing in the physical universe stands still, that as one door closes, another opens and that staring regretfully at a closed door causes weeds to grow through one's feet.*
- *The starting gate rises for all of us.*
- *The finish line holds glory and triumph.*

Start.

Start now.

Chapter Two

**Take
Inventory**

Skinny, Happy and Rich

Take Inventory?

What am I, a warehouse?

I have enough problems finding two matching socks or the gelatinous goop that keeps my feisty hair from looking like cotton candy in a NorEaster.

You want me to chronicle my life story?

Yeah, right—as soon as I finish this Bialy slathered in butter and my morning lifeline of good-to-the-last-drop. Maybe.

Oh, except that I can't. I have a list longer than Niagara Falls at high tide. Survive 480 minutes (but who's counting) of brain-drain in my cozy fluorescent lighted cubicle, fight with the knucklehead at the bank, pick up the rusted jalopy that moonlights as a housing complex for local rodents, and get back in time to greet the urchins, large and small, who gather in the family mess hall.

Take inventory? Sure, of the new tinges of gray that crept into my locks like crab grass.

What lies behind us
and what lies before us
are tiny matters compared to
what lies within us.

-Oliver Wendell Holmes

Does that resonate?

We toss rhetorical questions into the ethers like canned anchovies in a leftover Caesar salad, without any stomach to confront the generationally cemented *"truths"* that rear their seedy heads. We blurt out unctuous gems heard on talk shows as manifestos of great wisdom—the gospel according to Donahue—without ever pausing to reflect on whether these jewels belong on the treasure map to our Holy Grail of happiness or at the five and dime store with plastic strands of costume disappointment.

The classic (though not necessarily lucky) charms include:

"What do you mean it's my fault?"

Translation: *"I've been hammered on like a horseshoe at rodeo time since the day the stork dropped me into the lap of clueless caretakers. I'm not about to take a hard look at an obvious product of defenseless programming—ME."*

"I don't really want to know."

Translation: *"It took most of my merry youth to*

We have to be ourselves,
however frightening or strange
that self may prove to be.

-Mary Sarton

construct the fragile bubble of Fabio on a book cover in a Norman Rockwell landscape that I take refuge in. As long as the snowflakes grace the winter of my dreams with a blanket thick enough to mask my laundry list of pain, I'm too tired and scared to dust off the snow blower, fire it up and clear a fresh path. Maybe next spring."

"It's not about me."

Translation: *"The Madison Avenue composers of crass commercialism have splayed me like a squab at a benefit roast, stuffed me full of Air Jordans, Pokemons and more faux fashions than Imelda Marcos has shoes. How could I, in good conscience, claim ownership to my finely honed gotta-wear-Gucci needs?"*

Confronting the mirror for any purpose other than to apply disguises brings forth terror faster than a Labor Day barbeque breeds flies. What bar can we saddle up to and slug down a few shots of courage?

Even if we muster the fortitude, where's the check sheet? What program do I summon on my Palm? Help me out. Spot me the manual.

You argue for your limitations,
you get to keep them.

Fortunately, the Power of Truth lies in simplicity.

It is what it is.

Our environment, surroundings and circumstances paint a complete portrait of who and what we have become. We have brushed, splattered and spilled ourselves onto a canvas more rich than Monet's haystacks. Every thought, word and deed since the doc clamped the umbilical chord tells our tale of life in resplendent color, subtle shades, hidden meanings and obvious blotches. The lines etched around our eyes, the grays that bespeak our age, the hints of sadness that hold a permanent siege on our once smiling lips, open our window to the world. The raw, naked and savage truth screams out, begs to be heard and revealed.

Stop.

Stop and look.

The effects of your causes speak volumes.

Your job reveals how much you have invested in yourself.

Your relationships show your active commitment to others.

Your body exposes whether your health

*The ironic thing about life
is that most of us think we're realists
because we're so judgmental.*

promises hold any water or evaporate at the first sign of heat.

Your spiritual quest takes you down the inner path. Have you passed the first milestone or not yet picked an outfit for the journey?

Everything you have become exposes your history—HIS-story or HER-story.

You wrote it.

You revised it.

You chose the cast.

You played the starring role.

You scripted the current outcome.

Step back and re-run the tape.

Take a hard look.

It's all YOU.

*People judge you by your actions,
not your intentions.
You may have a heart of gold,
but so does a hard-boiled egg.*

Summary

- *The Skinny, Happy and Rich face their fear and use the mirror as a powerful tool for personal reflection. Rather than wallow in self-pity, pose as victims or attempt to cover the glass, the Skinny, Happy and Rich study actual results to gauge the actions that preceded them.*
- *The proof hides skillfully in the pudding.*
- *It's all around you.*
- *Look for it.*

It will talk to you.

Take Inventory.

Chapter Three

Take
Responsibility

Skinny, Happy and Rich

Okay, hold on.

First, you want me to take the most unpleasant step of mobilizing my tuckus.

Then I need to look at my meager accumulations, personal and material, and realize that they reflect my own development to date.

Now you tell me that I have to take responsibility for myself, my negative net worth, the forty pounds of donuts and Doritos packed around my mid-section and my string of failed relationships that make All In The Family seem like The Osmonds?

Whoa. You don't understand where I came from, the humiliation of three spinster sisters that dressed me like Barbie, the junk yard dog nun that whacked my knuckles with a wooden ruler and ran pre-school like a penitentiary, the parents who donned boxing gloves for weekend domestic disputes, the brother that put a tarantula on my curling iron and engendered an arachnophobia so

Skinny, Happy and Rich

ferocious that even Astroturf gives me the willies, a whole clan of cheese whiz lovers that clipped coupons to buy Ho-Hos and got to the end of the month too broke to even pay attention.

You expect me to take responsibility after all that? My trail of busted dreams looks like an Omaha landscape—flat, dry and endless. If finger pointing were a commissionable art form, I'd make symphonic conductor of the year.

Get a lobotomy, clueless in Seattle, they'll have a wet t-shirt contest on the North Pole first.

Focus on what is, rather than what isn't;
What can, rather than what can't;
What will, rather than what won't;
What does, rather than what doesn't;
What has, rather than what hasn't.

Response-ability, the ability to respond, to answer, to act in return—in other words, the ability to take one's own power regardless of circumstance and shape the outcome to one's satisfaction.

Go ahead.

Take it.

Take all of it.

Total responsibility means total power, for every condition or circumstance despite origin, flavor, protagonists, odds, roadblocks, adversaries, baggage, background or source.

No excuses.

Not now.

Not ever.

What pivotal slip on the slope starts us sliding down the path of denial and accusations? Where does self-reliance transform from mantel of honor into cloak of food stamps? Who greases the first skid?

Excuses spring like wildflowers.

"I'm a product of my upbringing."

Translation: *"I come from a long line of bitch and moan revelers, experts at complaining about*

*You can't build a reputation
on what you're going to do.*

-Henry Ford

everything, wizards of the blame and tell!"

"I can see that some of it is on me, but this other part..."

Translation: *"I admit that my high school years fell behind in a haze of partying and playing hookey. I guess I did gravitate toward such fluff courses as Material Science 101: Stone Tools to Transistor Radios and Clay Pottery as Therapeutic Relaxation in the two years I spent playing at college. Perhaps continuing education does mean more than lessons at Bob's Bowling Alley on Thursday nights. Still, I'm smart. I have strong management skills. That's why they made me captain of the Hangman's Noose Bar and Grille Rowdies for the third softball season in a row. I deserve more responsibility."*

"I can't control other people."

Translation: *"My underwhelming success stems largely from the gaggle of troglodites that masquerade as colleagues and don't pull their weight. One can't soar like an eagle in the company of turkeys. If I belonged to the right*

Whatever you've done up until now
is a manifestation of your beliefs.
It's part of your history—
HIS-story, HER-story.

bridge club, perched my hat on the country club rack—with a few friends in high places, I'd suck the public teat like a newborn calf taking to her mother."

Taking Inventory, builds the foundation for taking responsibility, one courageous act after another. With a clear and accurate picture, the observer morphs into protagonist, moves from writer into starring role. Written history, though already past, reveals in startling detail the lessons learned and those ignored.

All of us are 100% self-made. Only the successful admit it.

If we created our current reality, by definition, we can shape another for our future. 100% responsibility means total and absolute power.

We built it.

We can level it and build it again.

With every thought, word and action we define the road before us. We pave it on a daily basis, decide the surface, invite the potholes, set the speed limit. No one else can drive your ride.

It's up to YOU.

*A belief is not just an idea
that a person possesses.
It's an idea that possesses a person.*

Summary

- *The Skinny, Happy and Rich face their battles like King Arthur's Knights lined up for a Holy Crusade. They sit tall, heads high, in shining armor wearing full honor dress. Total Responsibility equals total glory. They accept no less.*
- *Allow the tragedy and weight of your life anchor you to the ground. Sink deep roots.*
- *Realize that the farthest you have ever been is only the beginning of how far you are capable of going.*

Your truth will set you free.
Your belief will set you on fire.
*People will come from miles away
to watch you burn.*

Take Responsibility.

Chapter Four

Make
A
Plan

Skinny, Happy and Rich

Plan?

You mean like Home Depot, Sears then bank?

Or should I get the bank out of the way first?

I've made plans plenty of times, like the last trip we took to the shore. We set out to cruise the coast line until the internet traffic report lit up like a fire truck at a five alarm. We whipped out the weathered map, found an obscure country road, shifted our plan on the fly. With Cheshire cat grins and the top down, we blew down Route 29 cranking Beach Boy Greatest Hits at 80 decibels, livin' large.

Until the tractor.

This corn-cob smokin' fellah in faded overalls sportin' a Massey-Ferguson hat rolled South at 22 miles an hour in a John Deere bigger than a house towing a crop duster that looked like a steel mosquito on steroids. He couldn't pull over even if he

Skinny, Happy and Rich

wanted to.

We sucked DDT fumes and ate shucked corn dust for 37 miles of country torment worse than a Hank Williams telethon off a scratchy AM transistor on a sweat drippin' August evening in Alabama.

Bad plan.

Oh, you mean a life plan? A yearly plan? With goals and targets and measuring sticks that chart progress?

C'mon. Get real.

A good goal is like a strenuous exercise.
It makes you stretch.

-Mary Kay Ash

Resistance to goal-setting changes skins more often than a jungle chameleon on the prowl, adapting and offering excuses like a Jewish grandmother defending her burnt Sunday meatloaf. Familiar creeds make the rounds.

"I don't do goals."

Translation: *"You can't make me and I'm not gonna'. I hated homework as a kid and hate it still today. I'd rather rack up demerits and go to study hall for adults (my living room of mediocrity), stare at the corner (in this case the television), pine away the hours fantasizing about the English teacher (or some Babewatch lifeguard) than take the time to make a plan and stick to it. I'm not in grade school anymore."*

"Goals don't work for me."

Translation: *"My two-bit job forms a happy haven for my continued poverty. Despite total lack of corporate appreciation and the favored pastime of trashing co-workers and bosses alike, I diss with the best of them, hide my battered self-esteem behind a fake bravado or false snicker and at the*

I know that most men, including those at ease with problems of the greatest complexity, can seldom accept even the most simplest and obvious truth, if it be such that it would oblige them to admit the falsity of conclusions which they have delighted in explaining to colleagues, which they have proudly taught to others, and which they have woven, thread by thread, into the fabric of their lives.

Leo Tolstoy

stroke of five, click my ticket and bail out of that hell-hole like Fred Flintstone fleeing the rock quarry. After that you want me to engage in a meaningful activity to create a new future? I'll get right on it after words of wisdom from Bart Simpson."

"Sure, I write out my goals. So?"

Translation: *"I spend the better part of fifteen minutes on New Year's morning in between hungover groans scribbling down the new me that kicks in as soon as I finish the last of the eggnog and truffles. I transfer last year's list (if I can find it) onto a fresh sheet, break it down into categories and give myself special permission to grieve my unachieved targets. Then I watch the Rose parade, call my best friend to commiserate and take a long Winter's nap. I've kept every record since 1972 and find comfort in the familiarity of each sheet, same goals, year after year."*

Okay, so it's hard. It's hard to make goals, even harder to pay attention to them, near impossible to stick to them. Except for one compelling factor.

Don't major in the minors.

It's worth it.

Every journey involves a destination and a map. In life, our goals represent the mile markers to our dreams. Without mile markers, we can't measure progress. We never even know when we get there. If we don't know we arrived, we can't appreciate the scenery, we fail to acknowledge our victory, we lose the opportunity to build self-esteem and walk around in the same condition that matches our mental state—LOST.

Compare these two scenarios.

Scenario A: I know where I'm going. I have a clear map, with specific goals that help me chart my course. I check off each milestone as I reach it, give myself an inner *"attaboy"* and strengthen my resolve to reach the next mark. Along the road, I learn to steer a better course, how to avoid potholes, when to put the hammer down, when to back off for better conditions. As a result, I develop finely honed driving skills that serve me in every journey hereafter.

As I cross the finish line I feel tremendous elation.

One person with commitment is worth more than a thousand with only an interest.

I celebrate the victory.

I internalize the spirit of a winner.

I anchor that sense of power within.

I enjoy the moment fully.

I prepare for the next journey, more confident than ever, secure in the knowledge that *"Yes, I can."*

Scenario B: I wander aimlessly at the whim of the crisis du jour. I have no idea when I actually accomplish anything because it was never defined as an accomplishment. Victories give me no pleasure, just another mindless turn in the road. I don't even recognize them. As a result, I feel no better.

My tires wear thin with each passing mile. There is nothing to strengthen them.

My gas tank runs on fumes. There is nothing to fill it.

Over time, I burn out, less than half a mile from a breakthrough.

It wouldn't have mattered if I had made that last mile.

Dogs don't bark at parked cars.

I wouldn't have known the difference.

I take away only scratches and dents from the passage.

Notice that in both Scenarios A and B, the physical voyage and precise number of miles traveled are identical, matching hills, rainstorms, heat waves, blizzards, flat tires.

Driver A used each obstacle as a barometer of progress. At the top of the mountain pass, she knew she was one range closer to the target.

Driver B simply felt tired.

Driver A survived a spin out, laughed, cleared the snow from the windshield, drove on encouraged, with another obstacle under her belt.

Driver B picked up a few extra gray hairs, moaned about the frost bite.

Driver A stopped her car at dusk after a monster heat wave, got out, pulled the bandanna from her head, wrung it out and watched the sweat sizzle on the asphalt, a testament to her victory. She had made it.

Driver B wanted a shower and a cheap motel to hide in.

Obstacles are those frightful things you see when you take your eyes off your goals.

Same journey.

Who would you rather be?
What's the difference?
Clear goals.

Happiness is an inside job.

Summary

- *The Skinny, Happy and Rich understand that the first step to getting anywhere means knowing where you want to go.*
- *The second step involves knowing how to get there.*
- *Set clear Goals.*
- *Let them talk to you.*
- *They are your friends.*

Make a Plan.

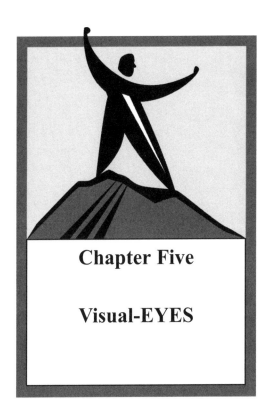

Chapter Five

Visual-EYES

Skinny, Happy and Rich

Whaddaya' mean "*visualize*"?

I have a hard time keeping the glasses straight on the end of my shnoz. The best image I can conjure is my Tyrannosaurus Rex employer throwing a conniption because some oatmeal-for-brains on the freeway decided to have a bumper kiss-a-thon with five other Rhodes' scholars (NOT) that clogged the arteries worse than dog hair in the kitchen sink after the first shedding of spring. I can see his toupee quiver in sync with his bottom lip. Does that count?

And where, pray tell, do I hole myself up in the dead of freezing to watch my mind's eye play Van Gogh? You obviously haven't lived the terror of a two year old slamming his infant sister on the head with the rubber mallet that genius Daddy left on the I-didn't-think-he-could-reach-it kitchen counter.

I tried the car. The acrid aroma of forgotten baby diapers under the

Skinny, Happy and Rich

passenger's seat and yesterday's McDonald's French fries drove me to seek cover in the dog house, the last remaining venue with any vestige of peace. I could hang with the cramped quarters if the fur covered blanket reeking of canine chased away the after hours chill.

No such luck. The ramshackle laboratory called home beckoned me like a lighthouse on a craggy Northern rock outcrop, surrounded by tormented seas and graves of dead dreamers.

Paint mental pictures? Hah!

If people can't see it for themselves,
they certainly can't see it for you.

As kids, we place envelopes under our pillows for the Tooth Fairy, cookies next to the tree for Santa Claus and carrots on the kitchen window sill for the Easter Bunny. We SEE these characters as real and suffer grave disappointment when later robbed of that fantasy by older kids that call us sissies.

We build racetracks in our Spaghetti-os with our forks, draw castles in the wet beach sand far more impressive than Windsor or Versailles—until unaware parents and impatient schoolteachers cut our daydreaming to a screeching halt. What a tragedy. As children we know instinctively that like the baseball diamond in Field of Dreams *"if we build it, they will come."* Adults become so conditioned to sight in the physical realm that we forget the source of uninhibited pure and free creation—the mind. We squelch ourselves and our brilliance, litter our sacred fountain with judgment.

Then we wonder why our dreams fade.

We replace our childhood promises with excuses.

*A person with big dreams is more powerful
than one with all the facts.*

"I don't get it."

Translation: *"Somewhere along this painful line I got smacked to the ground once too many times to dwell in Fantasyland. I made a choice to buckle down, put my nose to the grindstone, earn a day's pay for a day's work. I have no space for pots of gold at the end of multi-colored light refractions. I live in the real world, bills, taxes, kids to feed."*

"Can I do it on my way to work?"

Translation: *"I take my place in the rush-rush frenzy to drive 10 miles an hour down a highway, herded like cattle to a holding pen. If I can fit it in between the news, putting on make-up and Howard Stern (my daily fix for sanity), I'm golden. I can barely add a monthly stop at the nursing home to visit my ailing mother much less a daily routine. Do you have it in powder form, something I can slug on my coffee break?"*

"Who has time?"

Translation: *"Dawn to dusk I toil to make ends meet and manage my commune. I run the dog, ferry the soccer team, clean the house, fix TV dinners,*

Vision is the art of seeing the invisible.

-Jonathan Swift

attend PTA conferences, do my hair, catch a yoga class, chair the local Young Mothers' of America meeting, foxhunt in the fall and hop to garden club in the spring. I'm jumpier than a one-legged man stomping out a brush fire. The only place I find 'peace' is printed on a Christmas card."

Busy, busy, busy.

Rush, rush, rush.

Life ticks by.

Dreams, like the muscles in our body and the skin on our face, fade without exercise. Every day breeds a new compromise. We pigeon hole ourselves into tiny boxes with defined walls. We isolate into cocoons that never turn into butterflies. Day by day, we deepen the mud levels that keep us prisoners. We lose our edge, let our blades dim from razor sharp to butter soft.

In order to manifest in the physical world, we must first establish the picture of our dream in our mind. If we can't SEE it, we can't believe it. We can't make it real, chart a course to go after it or develop a mindset strong enough to carry us through the inevitable challenges that will greet us

The kind of winner you are tomorrow
begins in your mind today.

along the way. Without the mental picture, we fool ourselves if we believe our dreams will happen.

Here's the straight talk.

You have a dream which at the moment is too vague, like a fantasy. As a result, your actions to achieve that dream suffer from the same vagueness, like throwing basketballs in the general direction of the hoop without seeing the rim. Very few will drop through the net. Over an insufferable amount of time, at extraordinary personal expense, you may still score a few points if you throw basketballs until your arms fall off. Very few people have the stamina. Far better to stop shooting without direction, take the time to visualize the target in minute detail and only then resume your actions to score.

When you know the target better than you know yourself, every action you take will bring you closer to it. There will be no wasted motion, no mental gyrations, no errant passes. You transform from a blind pig rooting in the slop for a stray ear of corn, to a turbo-charged rocket with a laser guidance system.

When you have a dream
nothing gets in your way.
When you don't, everything does.

Spend time with your dreams every day.

Block out a space for yourself. Separate yourself from the grind. Close yourself off to do this exercise.

Think about your dreams. Experience them in complete detail. What do you smell? What textures shape the room or scene? What can you hear? Where do the sounds come from? What colors surround you? What furniture can you sit in? What hangs from your walls?

Now that you have the image firmly planted in your mind, add yourself to the equation. Let yourself go through all six senses. Stay with it until you own it.

Do this exercise every day, twice a day, morning and night. Go to sleep doing it. Your dream will move from the realm of fantasy into a minutely crafted vision. It will include targets and goals, concrete, specific steps which bring you closer each day.

If you can't see it, you're kidding yourself.

It won't happen.

Stop the folly. Spend time visualizing until your dream is clear.

The rest will naturally follow.

Success leaves clues.

-Tony Robbins

Summary

- *The Skinny, Happy and Rich accept that what you SEE is what you GET. They look deep within themselves, decide what they want, paint the image of precisely how it looks, feels, tastes, sounds and smells.*
- *Once they SEE it, they demand it of the universe.*
- *It always comes.*

See it first.

Visualize.

Chapter Six

Take
Action

Skinny, Happy and Rich

Oh, gee, you mean I really do have to get up off the couch after all?

Can't you see the value of lazy people? They're the ones who invented remote controls, electric egg beaters and those find-a-keys that sing back to you when you clap.

I'm one of those. Haven't invented anything yet—I'm in the gathering strength phase. I've had a few solid ideas.

Imagine a gizmo that sprayed a second layer of butter on the bottom half of a popcorn tub? I hate it when you get an hour into a movie and you're left with only dry kernels. Or how about a pizza warmer, like a tea cozy only bigger. That way, when Little Caesar drops off a double pepperoni, you can make it last a whole game without fear that the crust turns mushy or the cheese coagulates into those disgusting tiny rivulets of grease. I can't believe anybody eats that.

Skinny, Happy and Rich

Me and my blankie do so well doing so little. We've developed a bond stronger than Linus waiting for the Great Pumpkin. We're like Fred and Ginger, Bonnie and Clyde, Sampson and Delilah. Such a travesty for us to be parted over something so trite as forward motion. Isn't that for rocket ships that have boosters? Maybe if they attached one to my posterior I would motivate, too. I could use a scaled down version, become the Six Hundred Dollar Man. Besides, the world needs people who cultivate laziness as an art form.

How else could the rich and famous stand out?

*Genius is one percent inspiration
and ninety nine percent perspiration.*

-Thomas Edison

I wish we could devise a crystal ball to tell us when to simply listen, when to gently nudge and when to tee off with a swift kick in the butt.

I wish we could wind back the clocks and re-program every parent, teacher and ad exec that ever even hinted that we should take the easy road—a disservice more grave than imaginable to anyone pursuing big dreams.

The easy road only leads to places easy to get to.

You'll find no big dreamers there.

Most people do with dreams as children do at the seashore; they fill their little hands with sand and let the grains fall through, one by one, till all are gone.

Why?

Because they never start moving.

If you do things you don't want to do, AND…

You challenge things you don't understand…

You get results you've never had.

Most of us run more rackets than John McEnroe at Wimbledon. We kill our initiative with empty, learned rhetoric from friends, foes, critics, family

There are risks and costs to a program of action, but they are far less than the long range risks and costs of comfortable inaction.

-John F. Kennedy

members, television characters—none of whom live the life we dream about. Why do we listen to them? That's like asking a four hundred pound lard lover how to diet or a pauper how to manage your assets.

Stop it.

Stop and consider who you pay attention to.

This is your life.

What messages do you allow to slip in? Do they come from people you want to emulate? Do those people walk the walk or only jabber the talk?

We make it so hard on ourselves. Do you play any of these tapes?

"I want to, but…"

Translation: *"I've spent my life in a vicious cycle of never starting anything for fear of failing. Raised in a small town, my Mom and Dad never let me try ballet because it wasn't Joffrey, didn't want me to play an instrument since we had no Julliard, wouldn't send me to singing lessons because obviously no small town teacher could teach me to sing. I grew paralyzed from trying anything for fear that perfection might not be attained at the end of*

The best way to accelerate your success rate
is to double your failure rate.
The law of failure is one of the most
powerful of all success laws.

the first try out. At my first piano recital my mother told me I sang too high. I was seven and haven't hit a key since."

"It's hard for me..."

Translation: *"I come from a long line of whiners who instilled no values other than getting what you could out of wherever they were giving, settling for less on most any undertaking, putting down the pioneers who tried to break the mold and laughing at the miscues of those working their way up the ladder. They'd stop a parade just to pick up a penny and wonder in fits of self-righteousness why lady luck didn't drop a lotto winner on their deserving souls."*

"I wish I could..."

Translation: *"Somewhere buried too painfully deep to recall, somebody I cared about told me that I couldn't and stole my will. I've spent every day since looking for love in every place except the mirror. My self-esteem is lower than the water line in a drought and keeps me anchored in immobility like a supertanker short on oil. With each passing day of inaction my fleeting hopes fall like summer*

Get busy.

showers. I don apathy as my raincoat."

At the end of the day, action reigns supreme. All else pales by comparison. We spend valuable and necessary time and effort—the mental game—to prepare to do what we need to do, which is to get busy.

No matter what dream we hold dear, whether it haunts our mind or sits on an index card on our desk, only action will bring us closer to achieving it.

We already know what we have to do.

All of us do.

We just have to do it.

No amount of thinking about it will get the job done, regardless of how hard we rack our brains.

No pondering, no ruminating, no contemplating, no chewing on it.

Nothing will replace the simple yet awesome Power of Action.

You want your dreams to come true?

You already know what to do.

Stop thinking.

Just do it.

*Happiness is in the joy of achievement
and the thrill of creative effort.*

-Franklin D. Roosevelt

Summary

- *The Skinny, Happy and Rich don't waste time with empty promises or wishful thinking.*
- *They create a vision, make a plan and commit to it.*
- *Then they execute.*
- *No more, no less.*

Action makes them Skinny, Happy and Rich.

Take Action.

Chapter Seven

Track
Your
Results

Skinny, Happy and Rich

112

Oh, my Gawd!

Bad enough that mister cover-his-butt boss man forces me to maintain a log detailing every fifteen minutes of my scorchingly productive sojourn on company time, now you want me to fill out a check sheet on my personal goals and dreams? Why do we call them "*dreams*" if not to stare off into the distance fantasizing of a faraway land where men and women couple like tropical love birds, money truly does grow on trees and ice cream has fewer calories than lettuce? I have a hard enough time remembering to jot down my necessities on a list strategically placed next to the kitchen telephone for my weekly trip to Safeway and Rite Aid. You're asking for a multi-step process?

First, I have to pay attention to what I do.

Then I have to remember it.

Lastly, I have to note my actions in a sea

Skinny, Happy and Rich

of tiny boxes on paper that remind me of the crossword puzzles in the Sunday paper that I find so terrifying? To cap it off, you then want me to look at the totals at the bottom of the page and actually gage my progress, hold myself accountable?

Have you lost you marbles?

Perhaps you'll understand me better in Spanish.

No way, Jose. Basta. No mas!

*Some days you're the pigeon
and some days the statue.*

Yup. That's exactly what I'm asking. I'm asking you to stop fooling the person that's most important in your life, the one that suffers the most when you do—YOU.

Clear, measurable results tell the truth. Everything else speaks half truths, better know as lies.

Excuses pile up like logs on a woodpile.

They sit there waiting to be burned.

"I keep lists, been doing it for years."

Translation: *"When it comes to hardware stores and shopping malls, I blaze through those places like Grant burned through Richmond. I put one foot on the back of a cart and propel myself like a skateboard down the aisles. Before they even tally me up I've jotted my driver's license number and expiration date on the check and have my car keys in my hand. Not sure when I'm gonna get around to building that shelf in the basement for which I bought all this lumber but hey, I'm ready when the time comes."*

"I can remember it in my head."

Translation: *"I hide behind a false self that*

Some days you're the dog
and some days the hydrant.

masquerades as either bluster or low self-worth, justifying my busy life with a puffed up sense of self-importance, unwilling to confront the sad truth that I have no clue whether what I do and what I think I achieve match up or pass each other like two cargo ships on a foggy night, ne'er the twain shall meet."

"I tried keeping track of what I do. It didn't work for me."

Translation: *"When I recorded my activities, the wasted time piled higher than paper beer cups at Texas Stadium after the Super Bowl. The terror that swept over me like a tidal wave sent me burrowing back into my happy hole of justification and blaming the establishment. I love myself too much to go through that kind of abuse. Judge myself for real? C'mon."*

Face the music or watch the parade from a crowded sideline.

How can you tell the difference between activity and productivity unless you chart the results? How can you measure what works and

When you lose, don't lose the lesson.

doesn't work unless you track what you do?

You can't.

Period.

Most all of us have mastered the skill of convincing ourselves of either how hard we've tried, how strong our work ethic is, the depth of our desire or some other poor excuse for failing to graph our activities and dispassionately look at them. At the end of the day, best intentions yield little more than sob stories or pity parties. Hard-nosed as this may seem, too often we gloss over the reality that only certain activities give us results.

The rest waste our time.

Whew, that sounds so serious (and it is).

However, it doesn't have to be a drag.

Make it fun. Create your own personal scorecard. Write down the activities that you do on a daily basis to achieve your goals. Experience the joy and reinforcement of checking off your accomplishments. That's why they call it a SCORE-card—you get to check off a box every time you score.

Make living your dreams into a game.

Pay no attention to what the critics say.
There has never been a statue erected to a critic.

-*Jean Sibelius*

Play and enjoy.

As you train yourself to play, work becomes a game. When you win, the victory reinforces the process of training. When you lose, no big deal—it's only a game.

As you celebrate, you begin to develop the attitude and desire of a winner. You want to win all the time. This takes you back to the source.

Find out what works and do more of it.

Find out what doesn't work and eliminate it from the list.

Scorecards determine this for you—and they're fun.

We are what we repeatedly do.
Excellence, then, is not an act but a habit.

-Aristotle

Summary

- *The Skinny, Happy and Rich expend zero effort on activities that produce low results.*
- *Neither should you.*
- *To determine the difference between activities that serve you and those that don't, you must track what you do, examine the outcome of your actions and repeat only those that give you solid results.*

You want big results?

Track it.

Chapter Eight

Never
Quit

Skinny, Happy and Rich

"Never say die."

He faltered.

"Hang in there."

He hesitated.

"Keep at it."

He wavered.

"Tough it out."

He vacillated.

"Drive on."

He yielded.

The cries urged him, egged him, pressed him on.

"I think I can, I think I can," he mumbled to himself like The Little Engine That Could.

Wobbling and teetering he stumbled down the final stretch. He lumbered across the finish line, lurched through the tape strung by his loved ones, collapsed in a puddle of tears, joy and a sweet agony that only 26 miles of blisters rubbed raw and lactic acid could award.

Skinny, Happy and Rich

Eight arduous months for this moment of magic, an ambrosial drink of triumph over himself, how lush a taste, how rich a bliss.

He looked up at a lazy cloud hung in a pale blue sky and espied an angel winking down at him.

In the sweat that coated his lips he savored victory.

There is no elevator to success.
You have to take the stairs.

Our forefathers crossed the land in covered wagons. They braved droughts, blizzards and miles of open, empty space without a path. They outfaced savages and outlaws, weathered elements too numerous to mention, dared greatness to enter their hearts and carry them through. Following that example, generations of women and men with stalwart convictions challenged entrenched bureaucracy, small-minded ideas of prejudice and judgment. Many paid with their lives for the privilege.

Then laziness crept in. In the spoils of victory germinate the seeds of defeat. Fat, dumb and wearing a pretense of happiness we teach our children to seek the easy way.

"When the going gets tough, go shopping."

"Don't push too hard. You might wear yourself out."

The need to survive turns into a quest for comfort without effort.

We would rather watch MTV than learn to play an instrument, stare at a video screen than read a book, order delivery than stretch our legs for five blocks to pick up our pre-packaged food.

Accept the challenges,
so that you may feel the exhilaration of victory.

Except for one minor problem.

Lack of effort returns a corresponding lack of results.

The law of cause and effect fails to distinguish between the challenged and the gifted, the burdened and the fortunate, the wise and those relying more on moxie than marbles.

The universe doesn't care.

If you exert yourself, you define the podium. The extent of your exertion determines when you get there. The podium never moves. It waits, invites you to do what it takes to step up and claim your trophy, no matter how long the process, how arduous the journey, what obstacles confront you along the way. You set the pace and choose the rest stops.

All the while, the chatter rattles like pin balls in our minds, bouncing from one bumper to another.

"My feet hurt."

Translation: *"My mother wiped my nose as a baby. As a toddler, she picked up my toys. As a young boy, she shielded me from roughhousing. As*

Getting something done is an accomplishment.
Getting something done right is an achievement.

an adolescent she kept me from the bullies. I tried out for sports at school. On the first day of soccer practice they made us run three miles. My feet hurt. I quit. My mother understood. She bought me a trumpet. It made my lips sore. I left it on my shelf as a cap rack. It's still there today."

"It's too hard."

Translation: *"In a world of Kraft's Mac and Cheese and Orville Redenbacher in a folded microwave bag, I don't peel onions. I don't do dishes, hang laundry or wash cars. I take the freeway to town, bank at the drive-in and have a housekeeper that matches my socks. I end my work day at five, choose massage over exercise and use an electric toothbrush to pick leftover spareribs from my teeth. I let my fingers do the walking and know most delivery men by first name. If I miss it in the phone book, I can find it on the net. I see no sense in picking strawberries, milking cows and grinding ice ever since Ben and Jerry concocted Cherry Garcia. Call me crazy. I value my sleep."*

"Isn't there an easier way?"

Character is following through on a decision long after the excitement of the moment has passed.

Translation: *"I can't stomach the whole effort equals appreciation connection. I know myself. I'm an expert appreciator. Try me. All I need is a winning lotto ticket or a large inheritance and watch gratitude ooze from every pore. I'll spread it like an oil spill in Alaska, smear it all over creation. My grandma always said good things come to good people. I check my mailbox every day. Bring it on."*

Sorry, Charlie, that dog don't hunt.

No guts, no glory.

No tests, no testimony.

To merit that which you never had, you have to do what you've never done, over and over, until you get it.

With blinders anchored to your face and eyes steady on the target, march until your legs fall off.

Crawl while your hips still swivel.

Impose your will on those aching arms.

Force them to pull you across the finish line.

Your body will recover in a day.

You carry the victory for a lifetime.

When faced with a mountain,
I will not quit.
I will keep on striving
Until I climb over,
Find a pass through,
Dig a tunnel underneath,
Or simply plant my feet
And turn that mountain into a gold mine.

The world's congratulations won't hold a candle to the triumph that swells inside.

Own the glory.

Hear the music.

They're playing your song.

Never quit.

Not once.

Not ever.

Let me repeat that.

Never, ever, ever, ever, ever, ever quit.

Skinny, Happy and Rich

The greatest obstacle to progress is not ignorance but the illusion of knowledge.

142

Summary

- *The Skinny, Happy and Rich plain get it.*

  There is no free ride.
  There never was.
  There never will be.

- *Start.*
- *Take Inventory.*
- *Take Responsibility.*
- *Make a Plan.*
- *Visualize your success.*
- *Take Action.*
- *Stay Accountable.*
- *Never Quit.*

  Win, no matter what.

  Never Quit.

  Never, ever, ever, ever, ever, ever quit.

Postscript

Skinny, Happy and Rich

Think about it. In order to get anything done we have to start. We check our resources, consider honestly what we need, make some semblance of a plan, picture the end result, take steps to get there, measure our progress and continue with our efforts until we finish. No rocket science here. Most of us follow this simple sequence with routine tasks, almost automatically. Why? `Cause it works. That's how things get done.

The Skinny, Happy and Rich do more of it. While most of us use this successful process for mundane chores such as going shopping or planning a barbeque, the Skinny, Happy and Rich observe the same practice in embarking on a new venture, training for a marathon and turning their wildest dreams into reality.

Success conforms to a formula. Wealth obeys the formula. Losing weight abides by the formula. No essential difference separates the Skinny, Happy and Rich from the rest of us except that they understand what works and do more of it, in all aspects of their lives.

Here's the ultimate secret. You also know what works.

Take what you already do with commonplace tasks and apply the same logic to your life and all your dreams. You now know the formula.

Skinny, Happy and Rich

Crank your engine. Check your fuel levels. Decide that YOU can drive your vehicle. Chart a course. See yourself crossing the finish line. Put yourself in gear. Watch the miles fly by. Keep the pedal on the floor until the checkered flag comes down.

Read the book again and again until the formula lives within you.

Start. Evaluate your resources. Hold yourself responsible. Create a road map. Picture the outcome in your mind. Take action. Track your results. Don't stop until you achieve your goal.

Only you can live your dreams. In so doing you will inspire others. Teach them the formula.

They say misery loves company.
Success needs company, too.
Choose your company wisely.

Join the Skinny, Happy and Rich.

Skinny, Happy and Rich

Acknowledgements

The tapestry woven on life's journey blends its threads from myriad places, of shapes, sizes and colors glorious and brilliant beyond measure. I feel deep gratitude for the poets, prophets, mentors, taskmasters, pillars and light keepers that keep the path ablaze. I shall spend the rest of my days repaying the debt by carrying my small flame to the torch. To all whose influence shaped the ever growing mural I give thanks. My appreciation births its expression in learning to listen, challenging the arrogance that veils clear eyes and passing on what lessons find words to give them meaning.

A few special folk warrant individual mention...
- *Mom... it all started with you.*
- *Dad... for teaching me discipline.*
- *Siblings... my best friends for life. Neh.*
- *Giles... a brilliant educator who sparked a match.*
- *Unknown Va. TA... a grad student that saw promise and pushed.*
- *William Tazewell... for raising the bar.*
- *Anne Freeman... for keeping it high.*
- *Teachers at UCLA extension... for making it fun.*

Skinny, Happy and Rich

- *Ken Atchity... a kindred seeker.*
- *Henry... for standing by me, rock solid.*
- *janit... for believing, even when I didn't.*
- *Clark... for proving that friendship knows no boundaries.*
- *SGI members... for teaching me to never quit.*
- *Tim... for throwing me into the fire.*
- *Ron, Marc, Gina, Gary, Guy, Steve, Michael and the gang... we learned the ropes together.*
- *Upline and JMF... where the publishing began.*
- *CPG... a tireless team, doing a thankless job, building history.*
- *MLM Masters... who pass the knowledge on.*
- *Bruce... for the chances, the vision and the kick when I needed it.*
- *Aaron... for showing me what's possible.*
- *YEO and forum members... for the support and truth serum.*
- *V and T... for going long-term.*
- *Linus... for the window to the world through pure eyes.*
- *Camille... a bundle of possibilities.*

I love and thank you all.